This book is dedicated to the four beautiful and remarkable human beings who entered this world through my body and whose lives I had the privilege and pleasure to help build the foundations of: Luke, Josh, Micah and Kahlil.

A BUD ON THE VINE

The childhood memoirs of

Henriette Rosina Dorothea Maurenbrecher-
Fleischer

Born 20-01-1949

CONTENTS

1.

MY HERITAGE

'I am but a blip in time
a point on a line
a bud on a vine'

My ancestors, my self and my offspring are connected through the medium of genes and through the experiences that we have during our lives, which I believe can change our genes. Thus we are connected, thus we are one, and thus do we have the power to create the experience of those who come after us...

When is one conceived? At the moment your father's sperm finds your mother's egg? Thousands of years before that, as your ancestors pass on your genes from parent to child? Maybe I should start with the genes.

Northern European: Austria, Germany, the Netherlands. A little Spanish.

Maurenbrecher means "breaker of the Moors". Wikipedia tells me that, "in 711 AD the Islamic Arabs and Moors of Berber descent in northern Africa crossed the Strait of Gibraltar onto the Iberian Peninsula, and in a series of raids they conquered Visigothic Christian Hispania and tried to push further north into Europe. The term "Moors" refers primarily to the Muslim inhabitants of the Maghreb, the Iberian Peninsula, Sicily, and Malta during the Middle Ages. The Moors initially were the indigenous Maghrebine Berbers. The name was later also applied to Arabs."

The fact that my ancestors were called "breaker of the Moors" would imply that they fought and conquered them. It also tells us that for many generations, the Maurenbrechers were a military people. My father, Anton Arnold Frederik Maurenbrecher, was in the Dutch East Indies Army, rising to the rank of Lieutenant-Colonel in his forties. His father was a general in the same. His grandfather was a Dutch military man whose name we do not know. I know him only from a photo (2), where he stands in full uniform, a long, curved sword in his belt, reaching all the way down to the floor. Two large tassles hang from his left shoulder, and six medals next to them. A shining sash crosses his chest, and a black bag hangs low on his left leg. Polished high black leather boots make him look very tall. A thick moustache hides his mouth. A round, black military cap sits on the table to the right of him, covered in elaborate brocade. An elaborately-carved, upholstered chair is on his left. He is obviously a man of rank and wealth. His eyes look faintly familiar, like my father's... like my own. Behind the chair is the faint outline of what looks like a tropical plant, a palm of some sort, growing in a large pot on a colonnade. The photo is likely taken in Indonesia.

The uniform my great grandfather is wearing (photo 2) is almost the same as that worn by the Governor-General of the Dutch East Indies, circa 1930 (photo 1).

Photo 1. Governor General of the Dutch East Indies.

Photo 2. My great grandfather wearing almost exactly the same uniform.

3. My father as a young officer, standing in the left of the photo, at the wedding of his sister, Hannie in Holland, circa 1940.

4. My father as he was at the age of 50, just before he retired.

My mother also came from a military family, her father, Johannes Fleischer, also having a high rank in the Dutch East Indies Army.

Their purpose in Indonesia was to rule the people and get them to do what they wanted: provide the land and labour for the cultivation of crops that the Dutch could trade in Europe and around the world…. cocoa, spices, coconut, coffee, sugar cane, kapok, rubber. They also mined the gold and silver.

5. My mother's father, Johannes Fleischer

One can only assume that my family's military ancestors and their wives suffered much from their war careers, although those of rank probably suffered less than the humble soldier in the front line. But the suffering that my own parents endured as the result of war I know was beyond belief. Both my father and my mother were taken prisoner by the Japanese during their invasion of the Dutch East Indies in World War II. My mother lost her first husband, Jan Cox, during that invasion, lost her third child from that marriage who became ill as a baby while they were incarcerated in a suburb of Jakarta, and went into the concentration camps with thousands of other Dutch women and children with her remaining three children, aged 3-10. Thousands starved and those who didn't witnessed unbelievable cruelty and near-starvation by the Japanese soldiers.

My mother got herself and her three children through those four years of hell, but the experience left her and her three children damaged and traumatised. My father also survived the incarceration. After their release from the camps in 1945, my father, still a bachelor and 32 years old, searched out my mother, heard that she had lost her husband, and proposed to her within a year of their release. He became a good father for her two sons, Hans and Peter Cox and, for a short time, her daughter, Meikie. They remained in Indonesia, in spite it being a dangerous time when the Indonesian independence movement was starting and many Dutch were murdered. My father, being in the army, fought to keep Dutch control of Indonesia. Sadly, the third child, Meikie Cox, thin and frail from the camp experience, contracted polio and died at the age of seven, in my mother's arms, while she was seven months pregnant with me. In my little foetal body, inside my mother, I would have felt her grief and shaken with her as she cried over the loss of her second child.

My father's family were quite aristocratic, educated and cultured. My grandfather and father played the violin and all the men in the family became outstanding sports people and musicians.

6. My father, Anton, (standing behind table) with his family. From left to right: Hans (Henri), my grandfather, Hannie, Anton (my father), Wilhelmina (my grandmother), Joe.

My parents loved Indonesia, their homeland, with a passion. They spoke the simple version of the Indonesian language and had many Indonesian and part-Indonesian friends and family members. They had loved their life there before the Japanese occupation. My mother had servants for every task, including child rearing. On my father's days off, they swam, sailed, fished and hunted, all the time moving from post to post, staying only a few years in each place. Often they were posted to very remote places where there were few other Europeans.

7. and 8. Army patrol in colonial Indonesia.

9. My father (sitting) relaxing after a patrol

10. My father (bending over) surveying,
   supervising the building of a bridge.

11.   My father (on right) resting on duty

They knew and understood the land and the people so well, loved their life of adventure and bravely dealt with the tropical diseases and dangers. However, the history of my family in Indonesia was about to come to an abrupt end with the Dutch seceding to the Indonesian independence movement. My father stayed and tried to keep control for a number of years after the war, but was called back to serve in the Netherlands in 1951. My two older half brothers were already at boarding school there when my parents arrived in The Hague with my older sister, aged 4, myself, aged two and my younger brother, aged one.

Essentially, they were refugees, banished from their homeland. Holland was almost a foreign country to them, even though they had received their secondary schooling there and my father, his officer training. My mother hated the cold and the crowded city. She and my father resolved to remain in that country only as long as they

14

needed. That is, until my father was able to retire early from the army at the age of fifty. So, we lived in that one house in a narrow street in The Hague, at 136 Van Bevernink St., for nine years from 1951 until 1960, which is when we packed our belongings and emigrated to New Zealand. I was eleven years old.

I am not exactly proud of this military heritage, being a serious pacifist. I do not believe that the Dutch had any right to colonise and rule the islands of Indonesia. I can almost even sympathise with how the Japanese considered the Dutch and English colonisation in East Asia as a threat to their own self- rule. I take some comfort in thinking that the Dutch did bring some positive things to Indonesia such as their education system, health care, infrastructure and trade, which, although enriching the Dutch greatly, must also to a certain degree have benefited the Indonesian people.

Fortunately, I do have some ancestry which was not imbued with military history. My mother's mother, Johanna Vroom-van-Gestel, came from a family of printers and painters, among them a well-known Dutch painter named Leo Gestel, whose works grace many an art gallery in the Netherlands. She herself was a good painter.

12 My mother's parents. Frederika Louisa
Wilhelmina (nee Vroom v. Gestel) and Johannes
Fleischer.

12. The three Lanzing sisters. My great aunt,
Henriette Rosina Dorothea Van Putten-Lanzing,
(furthest on the right, whom I was named after)
with her two sisters. My grandmother Wilhelmina
Marie Maurenbrecher-Lanzing is on the left. Great
aunt Henriette was also a good painter and I am
blessed to have some of her work in my home
now.

My mother's father, although a military officer, was very musical and loved writing poetry. He cultivated my mother's musical and singing talent. She was an admired singer in operettas in Indonesia before she married early and had children. She always sang to all of her eight children and they all became good singers and instrument players. She also wrote a lot of poetry in Dutch during the latter years of her life.

My father was also musical. He played the violin and was a Bach enthusiast. When he got his first record player in New Zealand, we were regularly exposed to this and other great classical composers. But I never heard him sing. He was for some years part of an orchestra in Pukekohe, in which he played first violin. He was an engineer more than a soldier. He was very good with his hands, making lovely furniture, building boats, fixing cars and motorbikes. He also loved fishing and hunting and gliding. During his retirement years, he read prolifically.

This is the setting into which I was born. This is my heritage. Now for my mother. She undoubtedly was a remarkable woman and the greatest influence in my life. She determined much of my personality and physical characteristics. She deserves a chapter of her own. She is in my mind often and always stands over my shoulder when I have decisions to make.

2   MY MOTHER

No written description of a few pages can do justice to a person. So much will be omitted, so much incorrectly interpreted, so much coloured by my own nature and faulty perception. But here is my attempt.

Hendrina (Henny) Adriana Louisa was born in Tjipahit, Java, Indonesia, in 1912. Her father was a military officer in the Dutch East Indies Army. She was the oldest of three children. Her upbringing in Indonesia was problem-free. She was a healthy child, raised with the help of lots of Indonesian servants. As a young child, she loved to escape from the main house to the back where the Indonesians cooked the meals for the family and for themselves. She grew to love Indonesian food and learned to speak the "market" version of Indonesian. She was adventurous and loved the outdoors. She was expected to help look after her younger sister and brother.

As a teenager, she became a passionate girl guide and showed leadership talent. She went on tramps and camps and made close friends with other girl guides. Then, in her late teens, as was the custom, she was sent to finish her secondary schooling in Holland, boarding with a strange lady she didn't get on with who cooked Dutch food she didn't care about. She was miserable but studied hard and kept up her involvement in the Girl Guide movement. Henny showed a talent for music and became active in musical operettas. Her father was proud of her singing. She was slim and very beautiful. She hated Holland - its freezing winters, the dense population, the brown, drab houses of The Hague.

14 My mother with her fist husband (on her left) and her second husband, my father (on her right), in Indonesia, before the war.

15. My mother with her first born, Hans Cox.

Aged just 18, she met Jan Cox, a dashing young military officer. They married in Indonesia and at nineteen, she had her first child, Hans. Three more children (Peter, Meikie, and Kim) rapidly followed. She didn't mind. She loved children and had lots of help from the Indonesian servants raising them. All she had to do was breastfeed, cuddle and hold them when she felt like it. The servants would rock them to sleep, feed them, take them for walks in the pram, bath them etc... She spent much of her free time sewing. But she missed her adventures and outdoor life sorely, wishing she could go with her husband on the army missions. They moved every few years as they were stationed to different outposts, so she got to see a lot of places around Indonesia. Her husband was often away for weeks at a time sometimes. Tropical diseases were an issue. She had to deal with malaria, amoebic dysentery, fungal skin diseases, worms etc that lurked around every corner. During her husband's rare free days, the family would go with friends and their children to the beaches to swim, fish, sail and surf. They loved their life in the country they considered their homeland. But dark clouds were gathering on the horizon and life as they knew it would soon come to a sudden and traumatic end.

In March 1942, while the Second World War raged in Europe, the Japanese invaded Indonesia and quickly overcame any resistance from the Dutch East Indies Army. Henny's husband Jan went bravely out in a tank to meet the invasion and was promptly killed. Henny was taken prisoner along with thousands of other Dutch women and children. First they were kept in an enclosed suburb of Jakarta, several families to one house. There, her youngest, Kim, a baby of several months, became ill and died. Life was challenging and food was scarce, but the women were able to make and sell things, and trade the few possessions they had for food. Aged just 26, my mother had lost her husband and youngest child, and knew the meaning of hunger. Some of the women were taken away and used as "comfort women" (sex slaves) by the Japanese soldiers. Some were raped. My mother somehow escaped that fate. The women lived in constant fear and worry about their husbands. But there was much worse to come.

They were all eventually herded by train into prison camps. Henny's was in Jakarta, in an old prison previously run by the Dutch. There she had to sleep on the floor, in a small concrete cell with no windows, just a few metres by a few metres, with her three remaining children, Hans (7), Peter (5), and Meikie (3). In another cell lived her mother and her sister in law with her little baby (Hank Fleischer).

In 1945, after three years of pure hell, extreme hunger, and unbelievable cruelty from the Japanese soldiers who ran the camp, the war ended and Henny and two of her three children were freed. Her oldest, Hans, had a year earlier been sent to a men's camp when he turned 9, as the Japanese considered him to be a man at that age. That was one of the hardest things she has ever had to do in her life, letting him go, not knowing if she would ever see him again. But after the prisoners were released, they were soon reunited. They were skin and bone. Hundreds of thousands of women and children died in the camps from hunger and disease. Henny and all her three children had survived.

16. My mother and father after the war, with their first-born, my older sister Noes.　(Wilhelmina Marie), 1947.

17.　My mother and father relaxing after the war.

It did not take long for my father to seek her out and propose to her. They were soon married and in 1947, my older sister, Noes was born and myself, just twenty months later. But there was yet another tragedy in the wings for my mother.

18. My mother, pregnant with me, enjoying the last of her days in Indonesia. My half-sister, Meikie is holding my older sister, Noes. Just a few months later, Meikie died of polio.

When my mother was seven months pregnant with me, my half-sister, Meikie, aged seven, frail and delicate after her years in the camp, was struck down with polio and was hospitalised. She died in my mother's arms and my little body, unfolding in her womb, would have felt and absorbed every intense wave of grief and sadness at her passing.

Many of the Dutch and those of mixed blood fled Indonesia as soon as the war ended. Some returned to live in the Netherlands, but many emigrated to Australia, The US, Canada and New Zealand. My father was obliged to stay in Indonesia as the army was mobilised into trying to suppress the newly-fledged Independence Movement.

This was a very dangerous time for the Dutch in Indonesia. The Indonesian "rebels" fought a jungle war and brutally murdered some of the remaining Dutch. My mother, recovering from the trauma of the concentration camp and grieving for the loss of her first husband and fourth child just before this, brought my older sister, myself and my younger brother (Anton Louis) into this tense world. She would undoubtedly have suffered much anxiety during those years that she carried, gave birth to and nursed us during those last years in Indonesia. When she found herself pregnant with me, her sixth child, she admitted in her diary that she was "getting a little tired of having children". But there were still two more children to come. Contraception in those days was not talked about.

In 1951, the Dutch Government capitulated to the Indonesian Independence Movement and all remaining Dutch, including those with Indonesian blood, were expelled from the country. Thousands, including us, flooded into Holland which was still recovering from German occupation during the war. These colonial refugees weren't exactly made to feel welcome. My father continued to serve in the army and was promoted to the rank of colonel. Knowing that he could retire early at the age of fifty, thanks to his long years of active service in Indonesia, they decided to stick it out in this country in which they did not feel at all at home, planning to emigrate to New Zealand when my father retired in 1960. But oh, they were miserable there much of the time.

My mother found herself eventually in a three-storied, narrow brick house in The Hague with her five children. Her youngest, my brother, was just one year old. My father was not the sort of man who would help out in any way with the childcare and housework. In his free time, he would disappear into his workshop on the top floor of the house, or go away on hunting and fishing trips with his brothers. She did not have the help of her Indonesian servants now and had to do everything herself. But although she conscientiously practised her Girl Guide skills of keeping cheerful and cultivating a positive attitude in times of adversity, she found these years difficult. It didn't help when, in 1954, at the age of forty two, she found herself once more pregnant with her eighth child. On a mid-winter's night in December 1954, my sister Barbara was born.

3.

MY EARLY YEARS IN INDONESIA

As I was in Indonesia for a mere two years, I do not remember anything at all of this time. All I know is gleaned from photographs and stories told by my parents.

My birth was not straightforward. I presented with an arm first, and the midwife attending in that hospital in Jakarta on the 20 January, 1949, made me retract my hand by putting ice on it. Would I have absorbed, from this experience, a feeling of not being welcome... told to "go back in"? I don't know if she was successful in getting me to present head first, but I made it without any further complications.

19. My older sister and me playing in warm Indonesia.

Apart from the less than ideal political circumstances, I was born into a relatively happy family with two loving parents, one older sister and two older half brothers, who were at school in Holland at the time. My mother nursed me without any issues, and had those Indonesian servants to help. I had good health, although, as many others at the time, both my sister and I suffered fairly serious illness from amoebic dysentery. My older sister suffered more than me, apparently. She lost a dangerous amount of weight and in the months that followed her recovery, she was very fussy about what she ate. My mother had to spend a lot of time anxiously trying to get her to eat. I think I learned from that time on, to not expect too much time and attention from her.

This became even more so after the birth of my brother in 1947. I became that "middle child" who learns to amuse herself and not ask for too much attention. My sick sister and my baby brother needed it more than me. My sister was also, I imagine, jealous of me and was also quite temperamental. It was the beginning of me becoming a quiet, sweet, unobtrusive, helpful, self-contained child who was ready to please in order to receive her longed-for attention. They nick-named me "little cup-cake" (my translation of the Dutch word "taartje").

As for attention from my father, I just never got it and never expected it. He was never there. Noes received his attention because she was his first child. My brother Tony received his attention because he was his first son. I do have one faint memory of me around the age of 2, in Indonesia, being upset whenever my father went away. I

27

loved him so and didn't want him to leave and did not know when or whether he would be back.

But things were not going well for the Dutch. In 1951, they capitulated and all the Dutch and those of mixed blood were forced to leave. My parents packed as much of their Indonesian treasures (carvings, weapons, tiger skins, buffalo horns, valuable antique weaving, silver, ebony furniture) as they could and boarded the crowded ship back to the Netherlands.

4.

NINE YEARS IN THE HAGUE

There was family in Holland to support us, but they didn't live in The Hague, where my father was stationed. They lived in another town some kilometres away. After sharing temporary accommodation with other families, we rented our own house in "De van Bevernink Straat", not far from the coast of Scheveningen. It was a narrow street in a long line of streets, all the same, with three story brick houses cheek by jowl, a small yard in front, and a walled small garden at the back.

20. Our house in The Hague, 2018. Apart from the new windows and lush vegetation in the garden, it was the same as I remembered it when I lived there as a child.
I am in front, a relative's arm around me.

The street was cobble stone, with a generous pavement. This was our playground, where we played with the neighbourhood kids, once I got big enough. I have happy memories of hours of playing in the street. We played chase, and a game with sticks and bricks. We rode scooters and roller-skated. In winter, we had fun sliding on the ice on the road and making snow men. Our mother took us to some hills nearby (yes, they do have some in Holland!), after it had snowed, to toboggan. That was such fun. In summer we occasionally went to the beach to swim. We didn't have a car for some years. Later, I got my own bicycle and enjoyed biking around the neighbourhood.

We had many types of sales people who came along the street with their wares on carts: raw salted and marinated herring, a milkman who sold milk, yoghurt and rice pudding and man who played a street organ. That street was never boring.

One of my earliest memories was of gathering up dog poo in a bucket and taking it through the house and to the back garden, where I would be totally absorbed in mixing it with water and soil, enjoying the textures and smells. I wasn't punished for it and often wondered how I got away with that one.

That little back garden was mainly flagstone, but there were some flower beds with a few flowers in it. I remember being awestruck by the beauty of a very dark red tulip. There was a kind of tree with drooping trusses of yellow flowers I loved too.

21. In our back yard of the house in The Hague.
My mother, standing on the right, next to an
Indonesian friend. In front: me, my brother Tony,
and my sister Noes.

I loved nature. Sometimes our mother would take
us for a walk in a park, which was extra exciting
in autumn, as we would have great fun in the
piles of leaves lying on the ground. I remember
the pungent smell of the decaying leaves.

22. My mother and me in the park.

I went to a kindergarten for a short while. The only memory I have of that was being sent home to find a puzzle piece that the teacher had accused me of having taken home. I walked the two blocks back on my own, just five years old, not understanding why the teacher made me do this. I was quite sure I had not deliberately stolen the piece.

My older sister and I spent a lot of time playing with dolls. Sometimes we played "family". Other times we were "teachers". I became bosom pals with a girl next door. My mother was always "there for us", keeping us occupied and happy. She was a dedicated mother, warm and loving, but strict. I don't remember doing much with my younger brother and baby sister.

My mother, preoccupied with my two younger siblings, once didn't notice me going out of the house into the street, when I was just a toddler still. I was adventurous and walked far..... right to the next block. A policeman found me and brought me home to a very relieved mother.

Then, at six years of age, I started school. Our school was a kilometre or so from home, and we walked there at first, and later biked. Walking home from school was a risky business. Once, I badly needed to pee, so disappeared into some bushes along the road. I had my pants down and was squatting when a man suddenly appeared in front of me. I jumped up and started to pull my pants back on and he said in a friendly voice, "Don't put your pants back on, little girl". Needless to say, terrified, I did and ran away very fast.

One day in winter, snow was lying on the streets and pavement. I was walking home from school, past a boy about my own age, shovelling snow. I must have said something he didn't like (I don't remember). He went for me and hit me hard on the head with the edge of his shovel. I went home with a bleeding wound on my scalp.

The kitchens of all the houses in that street had a glass door that opened out into the back gardens. The doors had a marble step, and above them there was a window that could be opened and shut with a looped rope over a large screw. At my friend's place, next door, we were daring, and sat in the bottom of the loop and used it as a swing. I swung too hard and too fast, and the rope broke. I fell with the back of my head on the edge of the stone step and cut my head open again. I still have the scar.

That glass back door from the kitchen caused me grief in another way, too. I was about eight years old, and was learning to roller skate. The floor in the kitchen was concrete, and my mother very generously let me do a bit of roller skating there one day. Needless to say, I became a little too enthusiastic and ended up going through the glass door - blood everywhere and two nasty deep cuts in my right lower arm and hand.

My mother was very strict about not giving us any sweet food or lollies. I would see other children having them, and I developed such a strong craving for them. The Dutch are so good with confectionary. I would go into sweet shops and just look and yearn. There were lollies, but I particularly desired the lollypops, especially the peanut ones, the sweet and salty liquorice powder, and the chewing gum. My mother hated chewing gum, warning us that if it got into our hair, it would never come out. I desired it all the more. I had noticed lots of it on the footpath. I knew it had been chewed and spat out, but my longing was so great, I picked it off the pavement and chewed it. Needless to say, I was often plagued at night by a case of thread worms.

I am ashamed to say, that I also went so far as to steal money from my mother's purse. I only did this once. I walked to the end of the street, where an apothecary sold the delicious liquorice powder. I bought a sizable quantity and ate it fast on the way home. Once at home, I got sick and vomited it all up.

My mother was generally patient and understanding. But if she decided that you had been naughty, her punishment was devastating, for me anyway. Once, she had given me some money to go and get something from a shop (I don't remember what), and I spent it all on chewing gum. When I got home, she found the bag of chewing gum, and to punish me she made me stand for an hour in the corner of the living room. I was consumed with guilt, but my craving for the forbidden sweet stuff continued to torture me. How hard it was for me, when I had a teacher at school who used to take out a block of chocolate during class time and eat some in front of her pupils! The message that this conveyed to me was: "I have immense power. I can eat this in front of you and totally ignore your desire for my chocolate." Was it surprising that I chose to become a teacher?

Strangely enough, my mother once taught me an interesting thing about food. We were playing outside on the street one day, and one of my playmates was eating a stick of celery in front of us. My mother had never ever given us a stick of celery like that in our lives, and I was envious. I asked my mother if we could have some one day. She replied with a stern expression of disapproval of eating in front of others when they have nothing. Her thoughts, I imagine, would have visited her sad past in the Japanese prison camp, where watching someone else eat when your own tummy was gnawing with extreme hunger was torture.

Neither of my parents spoke much about the war and their experience of the prison camps in Indonesia. I have since learned that this is not unusual for the survivors of this horror. They want to forget and move on to better things. But there is one small story my mother did tell us. In the first few months of being in the prison camp, Indonesian people were allowed in sometimes to sell food to the Dutch women, some of whom still had some money or jewellery or some item to trade for the food they so craved. One day, a man came into the camp with a basket of eggs to sell. A long line of women stood in the hot tropical sun, waiting to get one or two eggs, my mother one of them. It was nearly her turn. There were only six or so eggs left. Then, to everyone's horror, a woman bought all of them! The woman standing behind her in the queue was so angry that she went up to this woman and squashed every one of those last eggs she had bought. The starving women still in the queue had to watch this precious food being wasted as it fell into the dirt and dust on the ground. This story made a big impression on me.

When I was in my fifties and my mother in her eighties, I do remember her talking about some of her camp experiences, especially when my half brother Peter (then in his sixties) was visiting. They would talk about some of the things that happened and my ears would be burning. Many of the camp survivors started talking about their traumas from that time in their eighties and nineties. Some Dutch women have written books about it. There is one book written in English by a Dutch-born naturalised New Zealander who wrote about her family's experience of the Japanese invasion and the prison camps. Her name is Ingrid Coles and her book is called "Two Slices of Bread".

All the houses in that suburb of The Hague where we lived had an underground cellar. This was accessed via a door from the hallway. As you entered, and before going down the steps under the ground, there were some shelves where my mother stored some food. I used to, from time to time, go through the door and nosey about the shelves, as well as sniff the musty, moist air that rose from the cellar. I enjoyed that smell. One day, I noticed a whole bar of chocolate on the shelf. My enormous craving once again got the better of my conscience, and I smuggled it out and took it to my little upstairs bedroom, where I role-played being a teacher and eating it in front of my imaginary pupils. The sense of superiority it gave me was marvellous. I don't recall being found out and punished.

I sometimes ventured down the steps into the cellar. Once, there were dead animals hanging off large hooks: deer and hares. My father would go on the occasional hunting trip somewhere near the German border and would hang the dead animals to 'bleed'. The horror of it fascinated me, and the beauty of the animals.... the tragedy of their fate.

23. My brother, sister and me outside our house, at number 136 Van Bevernink St. Standing behind us is Anneke, the girlfriend of my half-brother, Hans Cox. They married not long after emigrating to New Zealand.

I remember another punishment for a misdemeanour. I was enjoying my new found power of writing, at the age of abut eight. I enjoyed words. I had a little black board, and one day I took a piece of chalk and wrote on it all the dirty words I could think of (and they weren't that many). I felt a wonderful sense of satisfaction. But my mother was horrified. She punished me by locking me up in the toilet and telling me to stay there until she decided to release me. I think she was implying that I was full of dirty thoughts and should get rid of them in the toilet, but at the time I was totally perplexed. To me, those words were super interesting and I had no judgment of them being bad. But now I did! Plus, it was probably hardly encouraging of a budding pleasure in writing.

I don't have many memories of primary school. I know that the teaching methods were so different from what I found when I started Form 1 in New Zealand. We sat in rows and were totally silent most of the time. The focus was on reading, writing, and arithmetic, although I remember enjoying some drawing classes and some nature studies. I hated social studies/geography. It involved mostly the rote learning of place names and river names, which I wasn't very good at. But the three R's were taught very well. I was well ahead of my peers in my first class in New Zealand. I wasn't unhappy in school, and learned easily, but I do remember at times, looking wistfully out the window from my upstairs classroom at the tops of large trees growing in a park across the road. I remember being in awe of a large flock of crows, or starlings, sweeping in an elegant ballet across the sky. I longed then, to be free and moving like them.

I enjoyed many hours of roller skating in the streets with my best friend. We were allowed to venture beyond our street, into parks. During the cold winter, we also went ice skating at a skating rink, which I loved.

My older sister and I had ballet lessons for all those years we were in Holland. I just loved it and was quite good at it. But coming to New Zealand ended that. We also had swimming lessons. We learned only breast stroke. My mother would coach us at home, where she would teach the movements while we were spread-eagled on a "poof". There came a point, at the swimming pool, where we had to let go of the long "T" stick that the teacher supported us with, and swim out of our depth! I was terrified of doing this and kept refusing to do this. One day, our mother was swimming with us in the deep pool, and she just suddenly pushed me in! I swam, but I was so angry with her. It was such a shock.

My mother enrolled me in Brownies, which I wasn't hugely enthusiastic about as it was all so regimented and controlled. I loved being free and creative. I remember there was a big emphasis on getting "badges" for silly things like buttering bread, or sewing on a button. But I went, to please my mother. When I was ten, I received my first bicycle and I loved exploring the city in it, well, a few blocks away anyway. I biked to school and to Brownies.

One day, I came across a street fair, with merry-go-rounds. I was so fascinated by one of these and so desperately wanted to go on one! But I had no money. So, I was brave and, being careful to not let the man running it see me, I hopped up and sat on the edge of one and round and round I went, totally exhilarated. But the next thing I knew, I felt the sharp pain of a hard slap across my face. I learned my lesson: don't break rules and do daring things in life! Strangely, as an adult, I wanted to do exactly that, quite often. It was almost as a revenge, a statement to myself and the world that it was OK to do that sometimes.

There were some happy times with our extended family: grandmother, aunts, uncles and cousins who lived in another town called Naarden. We had family occasions, usually new years', or Christmas, at my aunt's place there. At new year's, we would be fed "olie ballen" (doughnuts with currants, cinnamon and icing sugar), and we would let off fireworks in the garden. I remember enjoying the smell of mulled wine.

24. At my grandmother's (Oma Noes) at New Year's just before we emigrated to New Zealand.

Once, we were visiting my grandmother, who lived with her daughter and her husband in this large house with a garden in Naarden. The garden had a small gold fish pond. My younger sister, Barbara, was just a crawling nine month old. I was five, and my older sister, seven. Barbara was left in the care of my older sister in the garden while my mother was inside. We were happily playing there, when we noticed that our little sister had crawled into the pond and, to my fascination, was crawling around on the bottom under the water. The next thing I knew, my older sister, Noes, jumped in and pulled her out! She had saved her from drowning.

I have a funny memory of visiting my two elderly aunts, who lived together in a house in The Hague. While there, I badly needed to go to the toilet to do number twos, and I did. Next time we went out to visit them, my mother told us children that the aunts had complained about the smell one of us had left behind when we had gone to the toilet. She told us we were not to go to the toilet there any more. I was horrified. What if I really needed to go? Would I soil myself?

At Christmas, my mother organised us into enacting a nativity play for family and friends. We each sang a song and dressed as angels and other characters. At other times, my older sister and I and my best friend would perform our own plays as well. I loved play acting. My mother put a lot of thought and energy into the script, songs and costumes, which she made herself. She also sewed beautiful little dresses for us three sisters when we were bridesmaids for a cousin's wedding. I was so enamoured of the white socks and gloves, (which we never had), the black patent leather shoes and the soft white faux fur trimmings. The fabric of the dresses was pink needleroy.

25. Nativity play. Left to right: Toon
(Tony), Noes, me, Barbara, my mother.

26. The three bridesmaids (with our
uncle Hans , my father's younger brother).

In Holland, people celebrate St Nicolas Day. We didn't receive presents at Christmas, but we did on St Nicolas Day. He was some sort of religious figure with a mitre hat and staff and a red and gold robe, who came by ship with his assistant, a negro, to bring gifts to the children of Holland who had been "good". We put our shoes in front of the fireplace with a little note. In the morning there would be a huge chocolate letter (first letter of our names). This was such an enormous treat! I wonder if St Nicolas would have given it to me if he'd known I'd stolen a block of chocolate that year.

I am seventy years old as I am writing these memoirs. All my life I have had a sugar addiction. After years of problems with my digestive system, I made a decision to give up sugar completely. What this brought up for me was interesting. Little incidents and the actions and words of others around me triggered in me an overwhelming sense of feeling unloved and ignored. As I was writing, I realised just how significant my craving for sweets was when I was a girl. One day, after yet another plunge into feeling miserably unloved, I suddenly made the connection. I had used sugar all my life as a way to fill the empty hole in my heart where I felt unloved. My parents weren't bad or cruel or neglectful, they were just too busy. I remember being hugged and kissed and receiving attention from my mother, but it was not enough. There were the five other siblings, my demanding older sister, my teenage half-brothers, my distant father who never helped my mother with any parenting or household tasks and gave most of his attention to my three brothers. And my mother was dealing with the loss of her first husband and two of her children, the trauma of

44

the war and concentration camp and her unhappiness in Holland. Is it small wonder I got very little attention? I didn't demand it. I was, most of the time, an easy, compliant child who kept fairly quiet and didn't expect much. But my sugar craving, I now see, was the result of a deep sense of feeling unloved. It was how I cheered myself up. It is what I used to compensate. Even though I know that both my parents loved me, they just didn't have the time to give me the attention I needed and do the things that would have made me feel loved.

27. My maternal grandparents' house in Soest, Holland, 2018.

Once we got our first car (a VW beetle), we did trips to grandparents more often. My maternal grandparents lived in a delightful two-storied cottage which my grandfather had built when he retired from the army. It was in a little place called Soest and sat in a lovely garden which I delighted in. It too had a little gold fish pond I used to sit by to watch the fish and the insects on the water. There were little, winding paths that disappeared into bushes at the end and it had a lawn. I loved that garden. I remember sleeping in a tiny bedroom upstairs. .

When I was older, we stayed over once and I was allowed to bring along my best friend, Erna. We slept in the garage which was attached to the house. Erna was very afraid of spiders and when one crept along the wall by her bed, she was very frightened and asked me to remove it for her. I refused, although I'm not sure why. I may have been as scared as she was, or I may have thought she was being a wimp. She told my mother about it the next day and I got a very disapproving look from her. That look had terrible power over me. She was good at making you feel guilty, my mother. I developed a strong conscience.

28. Grandfather Fleischer, my mother, myself, my brother Tony and my sister Noes in front of the garage behind the house in Soest.

I have another interesting memory of staying at this wonderful place. I was about eight years old. My parents, having just acquired their first car, and Dad having finished building a little sailing dinghy, organised a camping trip on the shores of a lake with other family members. In an effort to reduce the number of children coming along, I was asked if I would be happy to go and stay for a holiday with my grandparents in Soest. If I did, they said they would buy me a doll as a reward for giving up the camping holiday with my family. Always eager to please, and loving my grandparents' place, I agreed. I had a lovely time there, and the beautiful doll I was given gave me much joy, but I also always had a nagging feeling of having missed out on something really exciting and adventurous.

29. In front of my grandmother Fleischer's house in Soest. From left to right, (standing): My mother's brother, his wife, my grandmother, my father. On the ground: my cousin Robbert Fleischer, my younger sister Barbara, me, my brother Toon (Tony). My grandfather had died some years earlier.

Another way in which my mother controlled our behaviour was by telling us that every bad thing we did, God would know about, and he would keep a record of everything we did. He would mark a little black cross somewhere for bad things and a gold cross for the good things we did. I took it literally and therefore believed it to be totally implausible, so it never stopped me from being naughty. My mother was not a religious person, in the conventional sense of the word. But she did believe in a God. She became a theosophist just after the war. She accepted their philosophies of reincarnation, life after death, karma (reaping what one sows, even from previous lives), spiritual "masters" (of which Jesus was one), and the ultimate purpose of life being to reach enlightenment and "mastery" which meant one would no longer have to be reincarnated. And she did talk to us children about these things.

One of the 'naughty' things I did with my best friend Erna was to climb through the roof window of the top story of our house onto the roof. From there, we walked onto the roofs of the other houses and peered inside through their rooftop windows. It was so exciting. That was another thing my mother never found out about.

Erna was an important person in my life. I could always rely on her to be there to play with and we got on well and had fun and adventures together. But I also remember some awful fights. There was one, on the way home from school, where we got so angry with each other we physically attacked each other. Hair pulling and nail scratching and hitting! I felt so angry and so ashamed afterward.

I also did a very silly thing when I was about ten. I was playing 'chase' with a group of children in the street, which had concrete lamp posts on the footpath. I was chasing a boy I quite fancied, but as he was running away, he suddenly swerved. I cut a corner to catch him, not noticing that the lamp post was in the way. Crash! My face smashed into the concrete and I broke one of my front teeth. That accident led to all sorts of difficulties with dentures and false teeth later in my life. It should have been a warning to me, not to chase boys or men in my life. However, I did this twice, and twice it led to a broken heart.

One of my favourite things to play with was lego. I loved building just the outline of a house, with divisions for rooms. I would put in doors and windows, and visualise where I would put the furniture. We didn't have a lot of it, and my two oldest siblings and I had to take turns with it. I also used to love drawing house plans, with the furniture in place. I don't know why I never became an architect. When I was leaving school and thinking about what I wanted to do, I wasn't even aware that there was such a profession as architecture. All the girls went into one of four occupations: teacher, nurse, hair dresser or typist. Alternatives weren't mentioned.

My two sisters and I all are more sensitive than most people to bright lights, noise, smells, and touch. There was an incident when I was about seven years old which demonstrates this. I was in the dining room with my family. The weather outside was changing. There was a storm brewing. Suddenly, the house shook with a loud thunder clap. It shocked me so much I burst into tears.

I did not see or have much to do with my two older half-brothers. They didn't give us a lot of attention. But I do remember one of them, Peter, taking me to a ballet performance. He had a spare ticket as the girl he had bought it for couldn't go at the last moment. I must have been about eight or nine. I remember being somewhat overwhelmed by it all and finding it difficult to sit still for so long. Still, it was kind of him to take his little sister. Peter was going to art school at the time and was learning photography. I remember him using me as a subject to practise portrait photography.

The years flew by during this middle childhood, which overall must be considered to have been a mostly positive one. I had a stable, loving family in a stable, comfortable house. I had a very good friend in Erna, and was OK with school. I enjoyed good health and had many opportunities for developing such as swimming, Brownies and ballet. I loved ballet and was very good at it.

But the day was fast approaching when my father would be turning fifty and would be able to retire. I don't think I was terribly aware of the huge change ahead of us as my parents didn't talk about it very much with me. Suddenly we were on that massive ship called the "Willem Ruis". Many family members came to see us off. The trip to New Zealand took three months and I enjoyed my time on the ship, making a friend with whom I roamed around and explored.

30. On the ship to New Zealand. 1960. Left to right: my father, my brother Tony (sitting), a friend, my younger sister Barbara (on my mother's lap), me, my sister Noes. I don't know who the other couple are.

I was eleven years old, going on twelve. My siblings and I knew only a few words of English. My parents had a reasonable knowledge of English, from school and my father from spending time in the US during the war. It was a great adventure and we were supposed to be making a change for the better. My parents never felt at home in Holland, but to us children, it was our homeland and our time spent growing up there shaped us to a very significant extent .... greater than we thought at the time.

The year ahead, learning a new language (which we did easily and quickly) and adapting to quite different schooling and social mores, was tough in many ways. We had been uprooted, really. It was especially hard on my little sister, Barbara, who was aged six and had to start school immediately, not understanding a word of what people were saying. It was tough on my brother who was bullied for being "different". My older sister was much happier in her new environment, having been miserable at school in Holland. I suffered some negative social behaviours from my female classmates which affected my self confidence. I had always been a self-confident, almost cocky girl in Holland. In New Zealand I became a shy and moody teenager who found herself outside of the "in crowd". We were soon fluent in English and even excelled in English and other school subjects.

Another book could be written about my years growing up in New Zealand but this is where I will end the story of my early childhood in Indonesia and Holland, and the story of some of my ancestors.

Made in the USA
Middletown, DE
20 February 2021